# THE AMAZING LIFE CYCLE OF PLANTS

Published in paperback in 2019 by
Wayland
Copyright © Hodder and Stoughton, 2017

Wayland, an imprint of
Hachette Children's Group
Part of Hodder and Stoughton
Carmelite House
50 Victoria Embankment
London EC4Y 0DZ

Managing editor: Victoria Brooker
Creative design: Paul Cherrill

ISBN: 978 0 7502 9958 9

Printed in China

MIX
Paper from
responsible sources
FSC® C104740

An Hachette UK Company
www.hachette.co.uk
www.hachettechildrens.co.uk

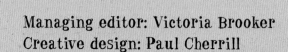

# THE AMAZING LIFE CYCLE OF
# PLANTS

Written by
Kay Barnham

Illustrated by
Maddie Frost

WAYLAND

Look around you. How many plants
and flowers and trees and grasses can you see?
Just like animals, these grow over and over again.
But how do they do it?

Get ready to dig deep and find
out more about the amazing
life cycle of a plant ...

A seed is a baby plant. It is wrapped in a shell to keep it safe until it is time to grow.

There are lots of different types of seed.
Avocado stones, apple pips and acorns are all seeds.

For a seed to grow, everything must be just right. There must be enough water, heat and light, as well as the right sort of soil.

When the seed cracks open,
roots grow down and a shoot
grows up. This sunflower seed
has turned into a seedling!

The shoot grows taller and thicker.
Soon it becomes the plant's stem.

The stem is strong enough to support the plant
as it grows bigger and more leaves appear.
It also carries water and food from the roots.
These will help the plant to grow.

The plant's leaves are very important. They take in a gas called carbon dioxide. When this gas mixes with water and sunlight, it makes a sugary food for the plant.

Now the plant has energy to grow.

The leaves give out another gas called oxygen. Humans need oxygen to survive.

Once the plant is fully grown, flowers appear. First, there is a bud. Slowly this opens to show the petals.

Flowers are bright and bold. They have a strong smell. This makes it easy for bees, butterflies and other creatures to find them.

Deep inside the flower, there is a sweet liquid called nectar. Bees use this to make honey. Insects drink it to give them energy.

As they hunt for nectar, creatures carry pollen from flower to flower. Pollen is also blown on the breeze. It is because of pollen that flowers make seeds.

It is important
that seeds do not fall
straight down. If they
land in the plant's shade,
seeds will not grow.

Instead, the plant scatters its seeds far and wide.
When seeds travel to many different places,
more of them might grow into new plants.

Seeds scatter in different ways. The wind might blow them away. Seeds might float on the tide. Sometimes, seedpods burst firing their seeds outwards.

Animals scatter seeds too.
When they eat fruit, the seeds hidden
inside travel right through them
and out the other end!

Did you know some trees and plants need fire to survive? This giant redwood tree does not release seeds until there is a fire. Then the heat makes the pinecones open.

Ash from the fire makes the soil the perfect place for a new tree to grow.

Plants such as ferns, mosses
and algae do not grow seeds.
They grow tiny, round
spores instead.

The wind blows spores away from
the plant. Some land in damp places.
And if other spores land nearby,
a brand new plant may
start to grow.

A plant's life cycle is the time it takes to grow from seed, flower, scatter seeds and die.

The life cycle of some plants takes just weeks. Others might live for a year.

The life cycle of the
Madagascar palm tree
is 100 years' long!

Plants' life cycles are very
important to farmers and gardeners.
Farmers need to know when to sow crops
and when they will be ready to harvest.

Gardeners need to know what
to plant so their gardens are colourful
all year round!

# THINGS TO DO

1. Grow your own sunflower! Plant the sunflower seed in soil and remember to water it. Then watch how tall it grows ...

2. Collect as many different seeds as you can and stick them on to a wall chart. Remember to label each one!

3. Make a colourful word cloud! Start with 'plant', then add any other words this makes you think of. Write them all down using different coloured pens. Start like this ...

ROOT PLANT SEED

# NOTES FOR PARENTS AND TEACHERS

This series aims to encourage children to look at and wonder about different aspects of the world in which they live. Here are more specific ideas for getting more out of this book:

1. Suggest that children keep a plant diary. They could plant sunflower seeds, then draw or take photos of the plants every day to see how they change and grow.

2. Ask children to decorate a paper plate to show the different stages of a plant's life. It could be any plant, from an oak tree to a pea. Then spin the plate to show the plant's life cycle.

3. Put on a plant life cycle play! Ask children to pretend they are a seed growing into a plant, before seeds are dispersed and the life cycle starts all over again.

4. Make a collage of a plant's life cycle using seeds and cuttings from the plant itself.

5. Search online for a time-lapse video of a sunflower growing from a seed to a flower to show children.

# PLANTS BOOKS TO SHARE

*Eddie's Garden and How to Make Things Grow,*
written and illustrated by Sarah Garland
( Frances Lincoln Children's Books, 2006)

*From Seed to Sunflower* by Gerald Legg
( Watts Publishing, 2014)

*My First Book of Nature: Flowers* by Victoria Munson
( Wayland, 2017)

*Nature Detective: British Wild Flowers* by Victoria Munson
( Wayland, 2016)

*Plant Life Cycle* by Theresa Greenaway
(Wayland, 2014)

*The Tiny Seed* by Eric Carle
( Picture Puffin, 1997)